God Is Here...

When Bad Things Happen

By Mary Martha Moss, FSP with Prof. Thomas H. Groome

Illustrated by Virginia Esquinaldo

Pauline
BOOKS & MEDIA
Boston

Library of Congress Cataloging-in-Publication Data

Moss, Mary Martha.
    God is here, when bad things happen / written by Mary Martha Moss with
Thomas H. Groome ; illustrated by Virginia Esquinaldo.
        p. cm.
    ISBN 0-8198-3102-6 (pbk.)
    1. Suffering—Religious aspects—Catholic Church. 2. Christian
education—Home training. 3. Christian education of children. I. Groome,
Thomas H. II. Esquinaldo, Virginia. III. Title.

BT160 .M66 2002
248.8'45—dc21

                                                        2002007315

Copyright © 2002, Daughters of St. Paul

Printed and published in the U.S.A. by Pauline Books & Media, 50 Saint Pauls Avenue,
Boston, MA 02130-3491.

www.pauline.org

Pauline Books & Media is the publishing house of the Daughters of St. Paul,
an international congregation of women religious serving the Church with the com-
munications media.

1 2 3 4 5 6   07 06 05 04 03 02

To my Dad, J. W. Moss—
Thank you for always showing me
the joy and exuberance of God's love.

Dear Parents,

This is a story to help children deal with evil and suffering from a Christian faith perspective.

To assist children who are living through difficult times, it is helpful to first reflect on your own reactions to tragedy. How have you felt when something has gone terribly wrong in your life? How have you responded? You may remember a particular personal experience and the fear and confusion it caused. Or, you may recall a more far-reaching evil, such as the Oklahoma City bombing, or the events that took place on September 11, 2001 in New York, Washington D.C., and Pennsylvania. How has your faith come into play at such times? How have you experienced the presence of God throughout? What have fellow believers suggested or modeled for you that helped? What has God taught you through such experiences? What is God continuing to teach you from them?

As Christians, we walk more securely with God when we anchor ourselves on a few core truths of our faith that can sustain us when bad things happen. What are they?

1. **God never causes evil,** whether it comes in the form of natural disaster or through the actions of people who wish to inflict harm on others. God has built freedom into nature and into people, and God always respects that freedom. Often we may be tempted to ask, "Why didn't God stop that person from sinning, from hurting others?" If God did such a thing, we would all pretty much live a "programmed" life…as robots. God gave us free will so that we could choose to love, to do good. Evil is the misuse of this wonderful gift. We need to pray to always choose the good that most fully nurtures life for all.

2. **Even when evil or suffering comes our way, God can draw good out of it.** Oftentimes when there is a tragedy in a community or a crisis in a family, we see people come together to support, to care for, to reach out to others in a way previously not thought possible. This is God's grace prompting people to choose good over evil, life over death, giving over taking. Jesus' resurrection is our greatest example of how God draws good from evil. Tragedy can help us clearly understand what is of greatest value in life: loving and caring for our family and our friends, and living as people of God.

3. **Suffering is not a punishment from God.** Our God is rich in mercy! We must always remind ourselves of this. It is true that our sinful actions can have consequences that make us suffer, but we can't regard these consequences as being willed by God. God never

sends suffering to teach us a lesson, since God's very nature is love. The Book of Job wrestles with the question of suffering from the perspective of faith. At the end of the book, God tells Job's friends how wrong they were to suggest that Job was punished because of his sin.

4. **Jesus taught us to alleviate suffering and to avoid sin.** Jesus wants us to reach out to all who suffer and to avoid sin at all cost. This means that with God's grace we can avoid doing evil and instead spend our time doing good in our own walk of life, especially helping people who are suffering.

5. **Jesus' cross and resurrection are victory symbols.** Our God is one who suffered for us and now suffers with us. In a paradoxical, mysterious way, death truly brings life. We believe not only in the resurrection of Christ, but that he rose to new life for all people. As Christians we believe in life and resurrection despite human weakness, evil and disaster. By God's grace, love is more powerful than death, and it always has the last word.

6. **Jesus taught us to pray for our persecutors.** He desired good for all people and preached that we love not only our neighbor, but also those who hate us and persecute us. To be

sinned against offers Christians an opportunity to be men and women of forgiveness and reconciliation.

Do any of these core convictions of our Christian faith pose a real challenge for you? What do you want to *do* to grow in these Christian attitudes? How might you share these convictions with your children? How will you pray for God's help and guidance?

God Is Here…When Bad Things Happen is designed to help you walk with your children as they grapple with the fear and confusion that evil and suffering may engender. The notes in the margins highlight thoughts and reflections that will help you share your own faith with your children. They also suggest activities to help children express themselves and to deepen their understanding.

May you and your child's journey in faith be strengthened by this story.

Sister Mary Martha, FSP

"Geronimo!" Jeremy screamed. "I love this game!"
"Me too," laughed Lisa, throwing leaves at her younger brother.
Suddenly, Jeremy felt a push. "Hey! Who's that?" he yelled.

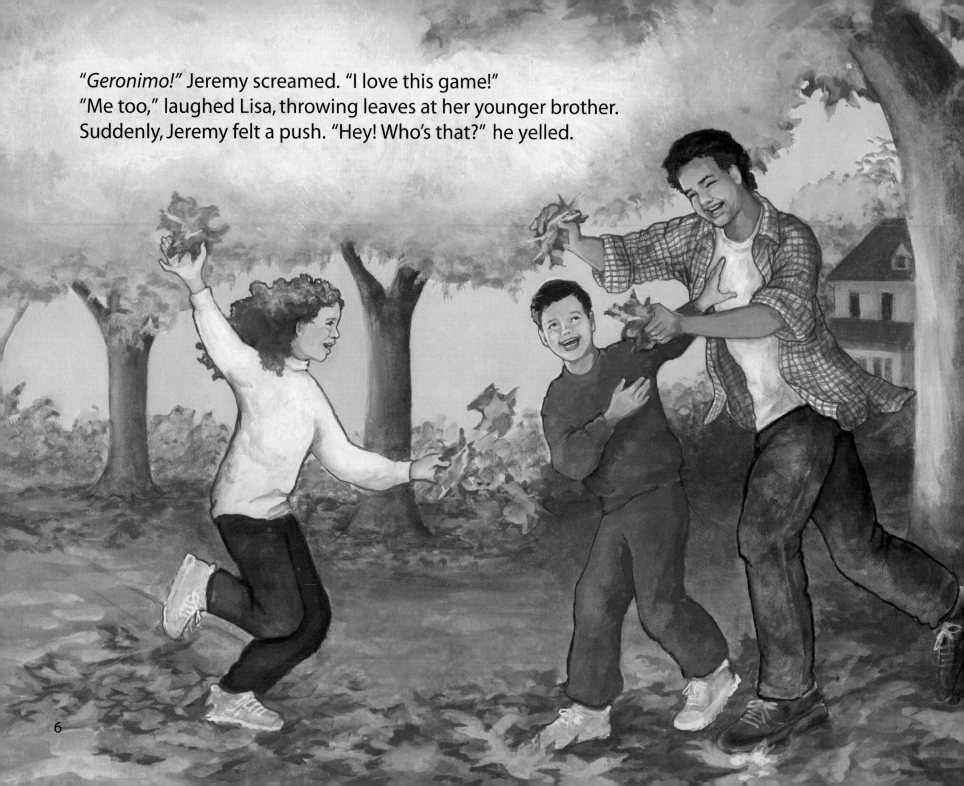

Enjoying the beauty of each season and bringing it to the attention of your children is one way to call to mind God's presence in creation. Seasonal holy days, saints' feast days, and family times together are other ways to celebrate God working in human history, in holy people and within our own family.

Help your children become more and more aware of the beauty of creation. Encourage them to thank God for the many natural gifts around them and for the gift of their own life.

"Guess!" said Miguel, dumping more leaves on Jeremy. Then the fun really started, as all three tried to see who could pile the most leaves on the others.

7

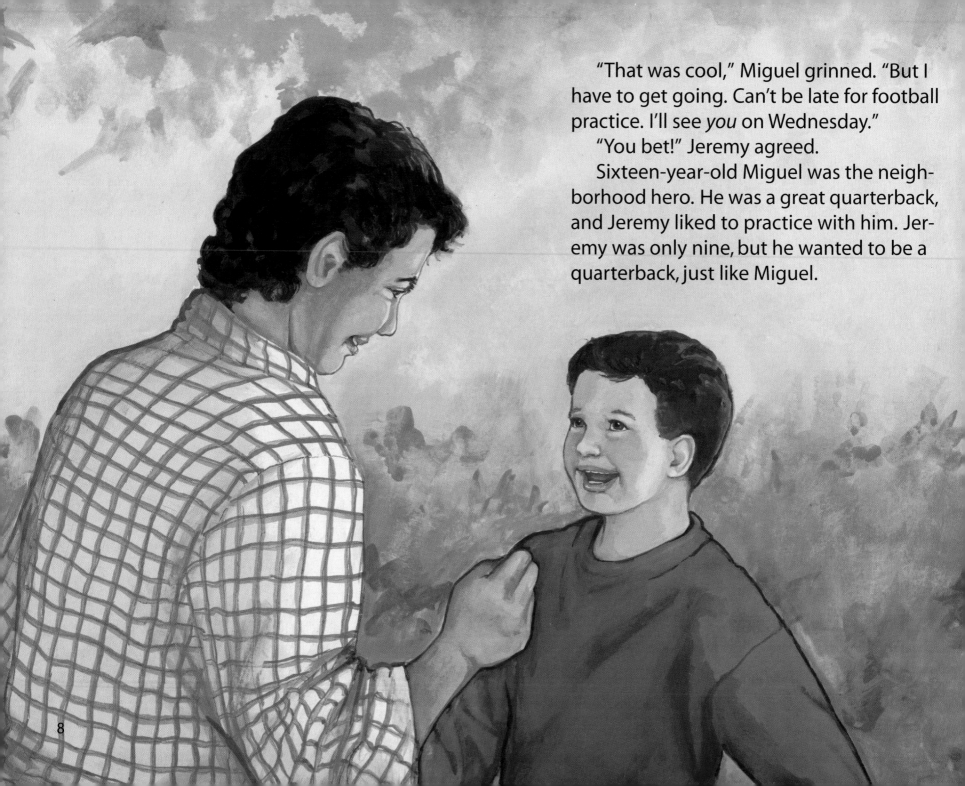

"That was cool," Miguel grinned. "But I have to get going. Can't be late for football practice. I'll see *you* on Wednesday."

"You bet!" Jeremy agreed.

Sixteen-year-old Miguel was the neighborhood hero. He was a great quarterback, and Jeremy liked to practice with him. Jeremy was only nine, but he wanted to be a quarterback, just like Miguel.

"Jeremy, what's this?" his mom asked when he came in from playing. "It's a seed that's supposed to become a vine," Jeremy explained.

"During religion class we acted out the story about the farmer who planted seeds. Some of them grew really big! Others just dried up. Our teacher told us that faith is like a seed…always growing. I need to water my faith, just like I need to water the seed."

9

How do you picture your Christian faith? Is it something that grows and gives life? Share this with your child. How has your faith helped you to become the person you are? How has faith made a difference in your life? How has it made a difference for others?

There are many ways we can grow in living our faith. Prayer and service to others help to keep our faith alive. Reading Sacred Scripture, even for a few minutes a day, can help us as busy adults to grow in spiritual wisdom. Sometimes we forget to nurture our faith, personally or as a family. Why?

How can you make more room for God in your life? Growth in faith should be life-long. God cares for our growth with unconditional love and constant grace…but we need to cooperate!

"Mom, how do I water my faith?" Jeremy asked.
"By doing faith-filled things," Mom replied.
"Like saying grace at meals and going to church?"

"Yes," Mom nodded thoughtfully. "That's very important. But faith isn't just about praying or going to church. It's also about being like Jesus, doing what Jesus would do."

11

Children learn best about their Christian faith within their own family. The more they see Mom and Dad actually living out the faith in everyday life, the more children will be "molded" in Jesus Christ. This is what the saying, "Faith is caught, not taught" refers to. "Being Christian" simply means to follow the way of Jesus in our everyday lives.

"What is something I can do today to be more like Jesus?" Discuss this with your child and explain why this is important to you. Invite him/her to join you in imitating Jesus.

12

"So," piped in Lisa, "when we make sandwiches for the homeless people at the shelter, or help Mr. Chan cross the street…are those faith things?" (Lisa was almost twelve. She knew a lot.)

Mom gave Lisa a hug. "Yes, Honey," she answered. "We do those things because we want to be like Jesus. We want to bring his peace and love to everyone we meet."

"Mom," Jeremy said in a puzzled voice, "do you think everyone wants to be like Jesus?"

"Why do you say that?" Mom asked.

"I was just wondering about people who hurt others, that's all."

"Sometimes people *do* hurt others, Jeremy. God has given us the gift of freedom. Some people use their freedom to do wrong things," Mom explained. "But God loves us and God can bring good even out of the bad things that happen."

One really powerful image of God's love for us is that of the Good Shepherd. Pray Psalm 23 to deepen your own appreciation of this image of God. Explain what a shepherd is. Speak about your own feelings regarding Jesus our Good Shepherd. Read aloud the story of the lost sheep (Lk 15:4–7) or of Christ as the shepherd who wants us to have fullness of life (Jn 10:14–18). Ask your child to explain how she or he imagines Jesus the Good Shepherd. What is Jesus like?

For Kids!

Draw your own pictures of sheep and a shepherd. Cut these out and use them to tell your parents all about how Jesus is our Good Shepherd. How does it make you feel to have Jesus as your Good Shepherd?

W hat do Jesus' cross and resurrection mean to you? Your own responsibilities as a loving parent often require that you "die" to yourself. Have you experienced resurrection after this giving up of your personal preferences? Jesus died and was raised so that you might do the same. Talk to your child about the meaning of the cross. It was once a symbol of shame. But Christ has transformed it into a symbol of love conquering death. Speak to your child about the power of love in your own life, of how love can bring new life.

For Kids!

Draw a cross, like the one Jesus died on. Or make one by gluing popsicle sticks together. Imagine that you are there with Jesus at the cross. What do you want to tell him? What do you imagine Jesus saying to you?

"Remember this, Jeremy: God always loves us and cares for us. And God is right there with us when bad things happen. God never leaves us."

Jeremy looked at his plant. He prayed in his heart: *I'll take good care of my plant, God. It will remind me of how you are with me, making me grow, not just in body, not just to be a good quarterback, but in my whole life. Help me to live like Jesus!*

17

How do you feel when people are violent or spiteful or uncaring? When you yourself are so tempted? Acknowledge your own feelings about this. How do we, as Christians, deal with sinful behavior? Do two wrongs make a right? How can you model your life on Jesus' when you are confronted by evil or suffering?

The next day at school…

"Jeremy, did you hear? The shopping center near Lincoln Park burned down last night! A lot of people were hurt pretty bad.... Some even died! I heard that someone set the fire on purpose."

"Oh, no!" Jeremy gasped. "I hope Miguel is okay...and Mrs. Whitney too.... They both work at the drugstore in the shopping center!"

Talk to your child about how he or she feels when someone is hurtful or uncaring. Ask why it is that others act in a mean way. Help your child understand that often these people have been hurt themselves. Explain how good it is to talk about things that hurt or bother us. Practice listening patiently. Ask: "Can you bring your worries to Jesus, your Good Shepherd? Have you ever tried?"

It was a very sad day. Many kids in Jeremy's class knew people who had been hurt in the fire. An apartment building next to the shopping center had also burned down.

Worst of all, *nobody seemed to know anything about Miguel.* Jeremy's stomach felt sick. He was very scared.

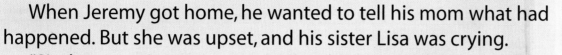

When Jeremy got home, he wanted to tell his mom what had happened. But she was upset, and his sister Lisa was crying.

"Sit down a minute, Jeremy," Mom said. "Your Dad just called. It seems that Miguel found Mrs. Whitney and led her safely out of the fire. But then…he went back in to help someone else. The firemen couldn't find him in time.

"I'm so sorry, Honey," she whispered gently, "but Miguel died in the fire."

22

No! Jeremy sobbed. His body shook all over. Miguel—his hero—was gone…all because someone wanted to be mean and burn down the shopping center!

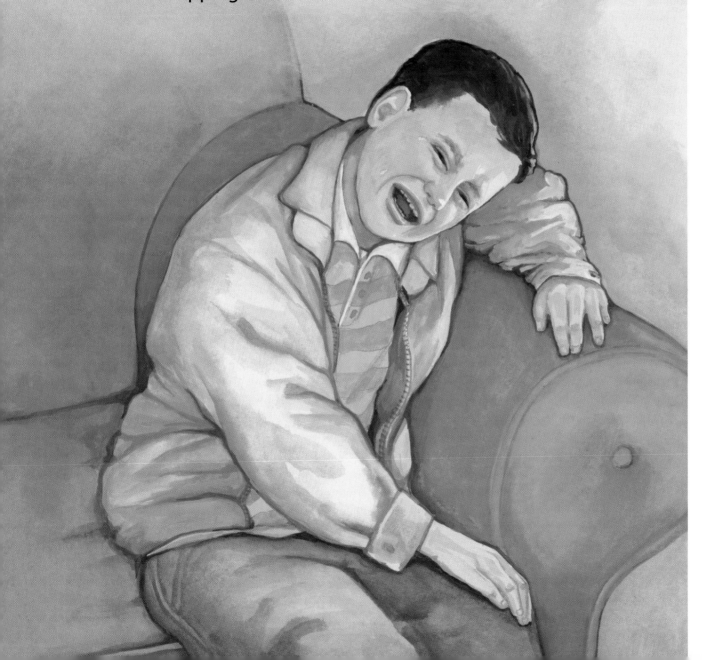

Bad news can provoke intense anxiety in us. Recall a time in your own life that was particularly dark or troubled. What aspects of our Christian faith helped you face such a time? Share this with your child. Explain how your faith has helped you.

Sometimes we feel very angry about the "unfairness" of life. Our children feel anger too. It is terribly important that children be able to bring such strong feelings to the proper expression. Encourage your child to draw a picture of what he/she feels like when angry. Gently talk together about it. Ask: "Can you tell Jesus how you feel?" Explain the difference between feeling angry and taking out one's anger on others.

For Kids!

How do you think other kids feel when they lose someone or something that means a lot to them? What could *you* do to help them feel better?

23

We all struggle with the mystery of evil and suffering…or why bad things happen to good people. Look again at the "anchors" referred to in the introduction. You might wish to do further reading from a faith perspective on these topics.

Dad came to Jeremy's room that night. "Dad, if God is God, how could all those terrible things happen?" Jeremy asked angrily.

Dad held Jeremy tightly. "Jeremy, God never causes or wants evil to happen. God loves us, but also gives us the great gift of free will. We can choose to do good things or bad things. If God controlled all our actions, we would be like robots. Instead, God leaves us free. Do you see how much God trusts us?"

"But Miguel is dead! People got hurt. And now some are homeless! What if someone burns down our house too?"

"It's okay to feel sad and scared, Jeremy," Dad said. "I know how much you hurt. We all hurt because of what happened. But God will help us take care of each other. In a very special way, God is with us right now. We are in good hands."

Imagine that your family suddenly lost your home or apartment. How would you feel? What would you do? How would you want others to help you and your children? What can you do to help others who are less fortunate? Talk to your child about these feelings and what you can do as a family to help others who are in need or suffering.

For Kids!

Jesus spent his life showing us how to live as his disciples. He especially showed us how to love God by loving our neighbor as ourselves. Who is your neighbor? Why do you think Jesus preached this great commandment of love? What type of good choices will you make today to be more like Jesus?

Help your child write, draw or say a personal prayer asking for something he or she needs from God. You may begin by posing a question, "What do you really need for *all* of your life—body and soul?" What about *your* own prayer for what you need? Share this prayer with your child, then pray together. Talk about the things you as a family really need and those you don't really need.

The next morning Jeremy felt so empty inside. He looked at his plant. "I water and care for you," he said, "but I don't see how you will ever grow. It's so dark down in that dirt. How do you even know which way is up? What if *you're* dead, too?"

"I heard you talking, Jeremy," Lisa said from the doorway. "Yeah, it must be pretty dark in there. I bet Jesus knew what it was like to be in the dark. He was scared when he prayed in the garden before he died. He prayed for courage and strength. Right now I feel so sad and scared, too. I need God's help, so I've been praying a lot lately."

Jeremy and Lisa looked at one another. "Maybe it would help if we prayed the Our Father together," Jeremy suggested.

"Good idea," agreed Lisa.

Jesus cried out from the cross, "My God, my God, why have you forsaken me?" (Mt 27:46). If we look at Psalm 22 we realize that Jesus' cry was drawn from the beginning of one of the most hope-filled psalms in Sacred Scripture. Turn to that psalm now and prayerfully read it, believing that God is speaking to your own heart. What words of hope stand out for you? Can you share this experience with your child?

The paschal candle we see by the coffin at funeral Masses is a symbol of the light of Jesus Christ given to us at our Baptism—the light by which we must try to live daily. The white linen that covers the coffin is a symbol of the baptismal robe we wore when we first "put on Christ."

Help your child to find the many symbols of faith on pages 28–29. What do these symbols mean? Discuss them or encourage self-expression through drawing or sculpting with modeling clay. Talk with your child about what she or he has made.

Father Jim celebrated Miguel's funeral Mass the next day. "Miguel lived out his faith in little and big ways," he told the people. "Even as a small boy Miguel would help anyone who needed it.

We all felt God's love through him. We will miss Miguel very much. At sad times like this, the first question we ask is, *Why?* But this morning, I want to ask a second question: *How?*"

Discuss what an apprentice is—one who learns how to do something well from another person who is a master at it. It is a given that apprentices are *learning*. Our Baptism is only the beginning of a learning process for life!

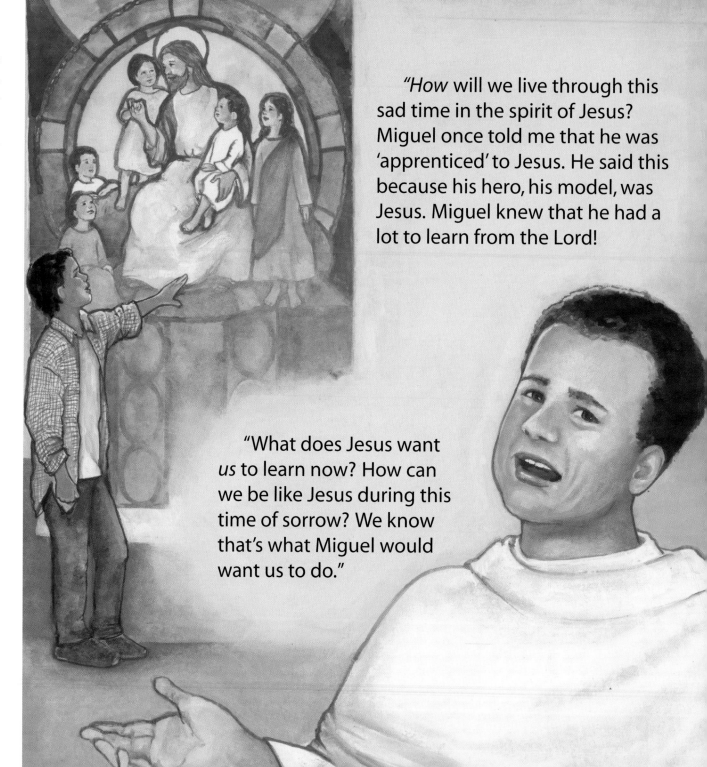

"How will we live through this sad time in the spirit of Jesus? Miguel once told me that he was 'apprenticed' to Jesus. He said this because his hero, his model, was Jesus. Miguel knew that he had a lot to learn from the Lord!

"What does Jesus want *us* to learn now? How can we be like Jesus during this time of sorrow? We know that's what Miguel would want us to do."

"In these sad and scary times, it's important to spend extra time listening to and loving one another," Dad said when they came out of church. "That will help us get through our pain and grief. God's heart breaks when terrible things happen. And God cares for us by having us care for each other."

Mom nodded. "Jesus taught us that unless the seed falls to the ground and dies, it can't grow into something beautiful and good, Jeremy. Jesus died and was buried…like a seed. He rose up to new life for us. With his help, we can always rise again to new life, even now in our sadness. And because of what Jesus did for us, we will see Miguel again in heaven someday."

Morning and night prayer and grace at meals are ways to support and pray for the members of your family. Such times can help your children become accustomed to viewing God as part of their everyday life. You can encourage this view by asking them during prayer times what they'd like to thank God for and what they'd like to ask God's help with. God wants to be involved in every moment of our lives, not just turned to in time of crisis.

31

Since Miguel is a person of Christian love and service, he becomes a sort of "Christ image" for Jeremy. Share with your child your ideas about the kind of heroes that can help him or her follow Christ. Talk about why these people are like Jesus.

As adults, we are learning each day how to be more like Jesus. Our learning must never stop, because we can always grow in the ways we live out our faith. Give your child personal examples of how you are growing and learning. Explain how mistakes are sometimes part of this growth. Share what a great adventure it is to keep growing continually in God, discovering new ways to love and serve more fully.

Jeremy was very sad that afternoon. "Our hearts are broken too, Jeremy," his mom told him.

"Yet the Bible tells us that 'God is close to the brokenhearted.'"

"Why don't you use your crayons to show Dad and me how you feel inside? Then we can take some time to talk about it. And we can use your drawings to talk to God about how you feel."

Psalm 8 speaks of the wonders of God's creation and the apex of that creation: the human person. Perhaps this psalm could help you deepen your own appreciation of the great gift God has given us—life. How does Psalm 8 help you to view the gift of life from God's perspective? As you pray this psalm, pay attention to what it says to your own heart.

For Kids!

Take a seed (for example, a marigold or grapefruit seed). Notice how small it is! Get some potting soil or dirt from the yard and put it in a paper cup. Now plant your seed. Be careful to give it sunlight and a little water…enough to keep it moist. Together with your parents, keep track of its growth. You might like to keep a journal that records how it feels to be a "farmer" and help new life grow. God's grace and love for us are like the sunlight and water we give to our plants.

After he drew some pictures and talked with his mom and dad, Jeremy went to check on his plant.

Wow! I can see something green coming up! I hope my faith is growing like this plant. If it grows, I'll be more like Miguel…and more like Jesus.

Oct. 29

Two weeks later…
"Hey, Lisa, I'm going over to see Mrs. Whitney. Want to come? I bet she could use some help."

"What about football practice?"

"It can wait. Miguel always thought of other people first. That's what I want to do. It will help me remember him…and be more like Jesus."

Recall people in your past who have impressed you with their love of God and service to others. Imagine that you could ask them to help you grow in one Christian virtue. What would it be? Why do you choose it now? How can you share with your children and others what that person of faith shared with you?

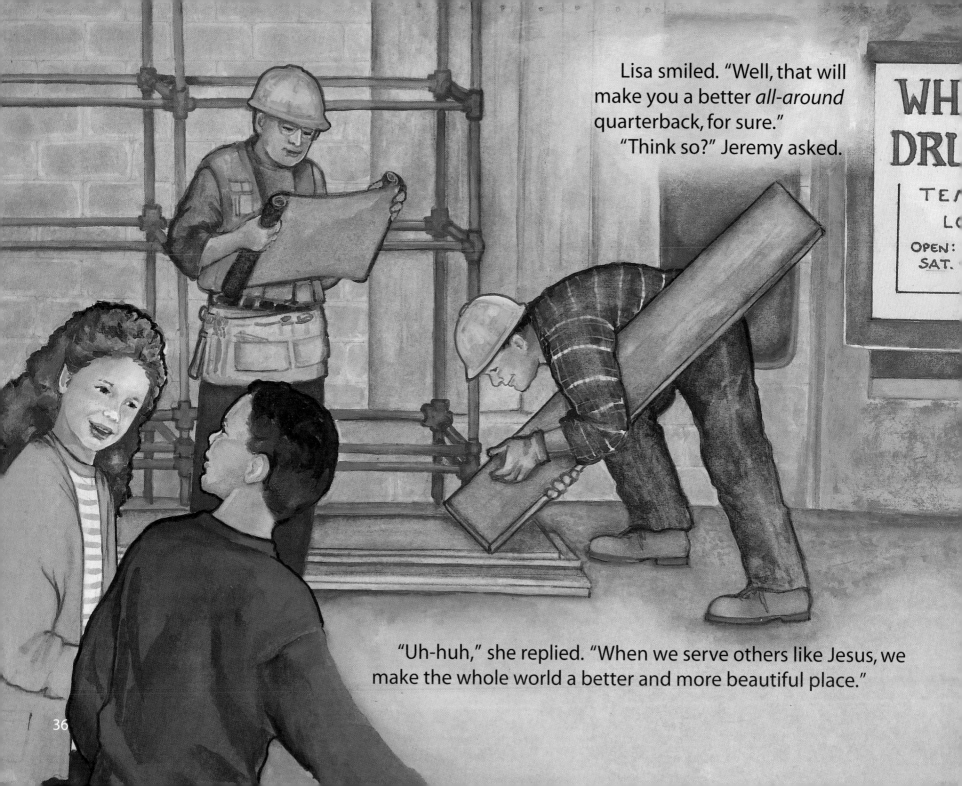

Lisa smiled. "Well, that will make you a better *all-around* quarterback, for sure."

"Think so?" Jeremy asked.

"Uh-huh," she replied. "When we serve others like Jesus, we make the whole world a better and more beautiful place."

Speak with your child about what Lisa means when she tells Jeremy, "…that will make you a better *'all-around'* quarterback…" If we are very talented and successful at something, but God has no part in it, our life will remain empty. Every person has a vocation, a calling from God, in life. What is yours? Whatever our talents are, whatever business or profession we choose, we can do it *for God* and *for God's people*, using our gifts to bring the world into closer harmony with God's dream for everyone—fullness of life in God's kingdom.

To Parents and Children:

This story is finished, but the seeds of faith continue to grow! You have shared about how bad things can affect your life, your faith, your family, and God's creation. Take a moment and share together how you feel about this story and the things you discussed together.

Go back to the first pages of the book. Read over the core convictions of our faith that can help you through difficult times. Decide which of these faith affirmations you want to grow in over the coming weeks. Ask yourself, "What can I do to nurture the seed of my faith, with God's help?" Imagine what your life will be like when you make a step forward in living your faith more fully. Use the closing prayer to ask for God's help with your decision. This prayer can be used over and over again to help you walk together through difficult times.

The Daughters of St. Paul, the community of sisters that published this book, accompany you with prayer. We encourage you to pray for other families who struggle when bad things happen.

A Prayer for Our Journey

Light a candle and place it before an object that symbolizes what you are struggling with: a picture of a loved one, artwork that expresses your feelings, etc.

Parent: God, our Good Creator, you are here with us. You share in our sorrow. We are afraid sometimes. We are sad sometimes. You understand how we feel. You understand all of our struggles. Help us not to turn away from you when we feel sad or afraid. Help us turn to you, who are close to us even in times of suffering. Loving God, thank you for always being with us.

Child: God, help us love and care for one another so that we may not feel so alone. Help us to be shepherds for one another, like Jesus, our Good Shepherd.

Together:

Psalm 23

You, Lord, are my shepherd.
I will never be in need.
You let me rest in fields of green grass.
You lead me to streams of peaceful water,
   and you refresh my life.
You are true to your name, and you lead me
   along the right paths.
I may walk through valleys as dark as death,
   but I won't be afraid.
You are with me, and your shepherd's rod
   makes me feel safe.
You treat me to a feast, while my enemies
   watch.
You honor me as your guest, and you fill my
   cup until it overflows.
Your kindness and love will always be with
   me each day of my life,
and I will live forever
   in your house, Lord.
[CEV Bible]

Pauline
BOOKS & MEDIA

The Daughters of St. Paul operate book and media centers at the following addresses. Visit, call or write the one nearest you today, or find us on the World Wide Web, www.pauline.org

CALIFORNIA
3908 Sepulveda Blvd, Culver City, CA 90230 — 310-397-8676
5945 Balboa Avenue, San Diego, CA 92111 — 858-565-9181
46 Geary Street, San Francisco, CA 94108 — 415-781-5180

FLORIDA
145 S.W. 107th Avenue, Miami, FL 33174 — 305-559-6715

HAWAII
1143 Bishop Street, Honolulu, HI 96813 — 808-521-2731
Neighbor Islands call: 800-259-8463

ILLINOIS
172 North Michigan Avenue, Chicago, IL 60601 — 312-346-4228

LOUISIANA
4403 Veterans Memorial Blvd, Metairie, LA 70006 — 504-887-7631

MASSACHUSETTS
885 Providence Hwy, Dedham, MA 02026 — 781-326-5385

MISSOURI
9804 Watson Road, St. Louis, MO 63126 — 314-965-3512

NEW JERSEY
561 U.S. Route 1, Wick Plaza, Edison, NJ 08817 — 732-572-1200

NEW YORK
150 East 52nd Street, New York, NY 10022 — 212-754-1110
78 Fort Place, Staten Island, NY 10301 — 718-447-5071

PENNSYLVANIA
9171-A Roosevelt Blvd, Philadelphia, PA 19114 — 215-676-9494

SOUTH CAROLINA
243 King Street, Charleston, SC 29401 — 843-577-0175

TENNESSEE
4811 Poplar Avenue, Memphis, TN 38117 — 901-761-2987

TEXAS
114 Main Plaza, San Antonio, TX 78205 — 210-224-8101

VIRGINIA
1025 King Street, Alexandria, VA 22314 — 703-549-3806

CANADA
3022 Dufferin Street, Toronto, Ontario, Canada M6B 3T5 — 416-781-9131
1155 Yonge Street, Toronto, Ontario, Canada M4T 1W2 — 416-934-3440

¡También somos su fuente para libros, videos y música en español!